THE LAWS OF MOTION

PHYSICS FOR KIDS

Children's Physics Books

Speedy Publishing LLC
40 E. Main St. #1156
Newark, DE 19711
www.speedypublishing.com

n this book, we're going to talk about Newton's Laws of Motion. So, let's get right to it!

For many centuries, philosophers created theories about the physical nature of the universe. However, it wasn't until scientists began to use scientific methods that theories could be tested to see if they were true or not.

Newton's Cradle executive toy in motion.

WHO WAS ISAAC NEWTON?

The famous British physicist Sir Isaac Newton was born in 1642 and became one of the greatest physicists throughout history.

Three notable scientists who came before him were:

- Archimedes of Syracuse, a Greek mathematician, inventor, physicist, and astronomer, who inspired both Newton and Galileo to explore the mathematics of motion.

- Copernicus, a Polish astronomer and physicist, who stated that the sun, not the Earth, was at the center of the universe

Archimedes engraving 1881.

- Galileo Galilei, an Italian mathematician, physicist, astronomer, engineer, and philosopher who was the first person to use a telescope and who confirmed the theories of Copernicus

Astronomer Nicolaus Copernicus from 1877.

Newton once acknowledged that he was standing on the shoulders of the scientific "giants" who had come before him when he did his work. By this, Newton meant that the great scientists who came before him, such as Archimedes, Copernicus, and Galileo, made it possible for him to achieve what he did in his chosen field. He was able to see farther than others into the mysteries of physics, because he was using the work that the other "giants" in his field had published.

Newton's law of motion concept.

NEWTONS LAW OF MOTION

$$F = ma \qquad -3N$$

F = FORCE APPIED

m = mass of body

a = body's accelerat

$$F_1 + F_2 + \cdots F_n = F_{net} = m$$

$$F_{net} = ma = m\frac{dv}{dt} = \frac{d(m}{d}$$

$$F_{net} = \frac{dp}{dt}$$

$$I = \int_{\Delta t} F\, dt$$

$$I = \Delta P = m\,\Delta p = m$$

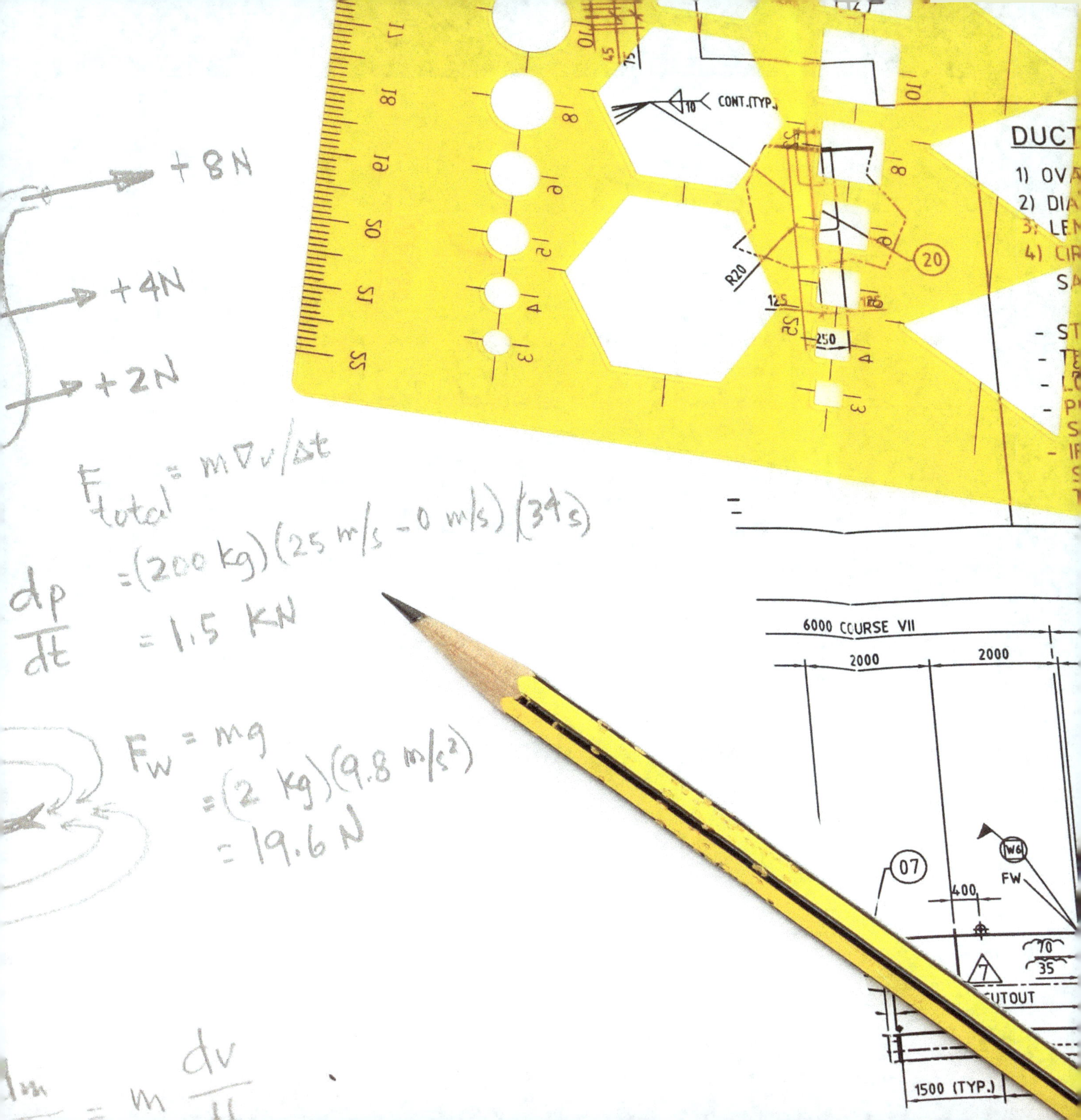

+8N
+4N
+2N
F_total = mΔv/Δt
= (200 kg)(25 m/s - 0 m/s)(3 4 s)
dp/dt = 1.5 KN
F_W = mg
= (2 kg)(9.8 m/s²)
= 19.6 N
= m dv/dt
10
CONT. (TYP.)
R20
20
125
250
DUCT
1) OVA
2) DIA
3) LEN
4) CIR
SA
ST
6000 COURSE VII
2000
2000
07
W6
FW
400
70
35
CUTOUT
1500 (TYP.)

WHEN DID ISAAC NEWTON PUBLISH HIS LAWS OF MOTION?

Like Archimedes, Copernicus, and Galileo before him, Newton began his study of motion by observing the movements of the planets. He wanted to determine how these huge objects would react when forces such as gravity influenced them. Even though other scientists used the scientific method to show evidence of their work, Newton refined the scientific method into a system that scientists still use today.

The Greek Philosopher Aristotle had proposed a description of the motions that took place within the physical universe. He explained these as a set of natural motions and a set of violent motions. Natural motions are motions that happened without human intervention. For example, smoke from a fire naturally rises. *"Violent"* motions didn't mean violence in the way we think of it.

Instead, it just meant that the motion was caused by a person or other force. For example, if you throw a ball in the air to make a basket or you take a whisk to beat up some batter. These actions would fall in the category of *"violent"* force.

There were many issues with Aristotle's theories and little by little his theories on motion were dismantled. Newton began to study, experiment, and record his findings. He published a book in 1687 called the Mathematical Principles of Natural Philosophy.

Sir Isaac Newton.

Newton's three laws of motion were described in his book. He also explained his theories concerning gravity. Many scientists, including the famous physicist Albert Einstein, felt that Newton's book was the most important scientific book ever published.

Famous scientists: Gutenberg, Newton, Galilei, Humboldt, wood engraving, published 1876.

J. GUTTENBERG.
I. NEWTON
G. GALILEI.
A. V. HUMBOLDT.

The three laws of motion that Newton formulated might seem like common sense to you, because you can see evidence of them all around you. However, when these laws were first explained to the scientific community they created a revolution and were the start of the study of modern physics.

Engraving of physicist Isaac Newton from 1881.

I Got IT!

WHAT IS FORCE?

In order to understand Newton's laws of motion, you need to understand what a force is. A force is some action that is taken that affects the state of an object's motion. For example, let's say that you and your Dad are playing a game of catch in the backyard. When your Dad throws the ball at you, he's exerting a force to do so. That force acts on the ball and makes it move.

To explain force, we use the strength of the force, but we also use its direction. In other words, the direction your Dad is throwing the ball, toward you, has an impact on the flight path of the object he's trying to move—the ball. The harder he throws the ball, the farther it will travel. Forces exist every where on Earth. Sometimes forces aren't that easy to see. For example, the force of gravity keeps us from floating off the Earth's surface.

Father and teenage son playing baseball.

Newton's First Law of Motion

Drag

NEWTON'S FIRST LAW OF MOTION

In simple terms, Newton's first law states that if an object is at rest, it's going to stay that way unless something happens to change it. In other words, if you're holding a softball in your mitt and it's just sitting there, that won't change unless you apply some force to it and throw it to get it to travel in the air.

How far, how fast, and in which direction it travels will depend on the amount of force you apply to it, as well as the direction of that force. When an object remains at rest, because no force is acting on it, it's in a state of "inertia." It doesn't start moving all by itself. Some force has to be applied to it.

The first law also says that objects will maintain their speed and direction, which is their velocity, unless an unbalanced force comes along to change their movement. In our everyday life this isn't easy to see. The reason is that there are a lot of unforeseen forces on Earth that are acting on the object. The friction of the atmosphere and the gravity of Earth both have an impact on the object.

Newton's law of motion.

F=ma

Imagine that you and your Dad are suspended in space and there are no large planets to pull on your softball. If you miss catching the softball when he throws it, it would just keep traveling in a straight line with the same speed and direction as when he threw it. The velocity of the softball is its speed in a certain direction. So, in other words, we can say that the softball will keep its velocity.

Fast Ball.

Of course, if it hit an asteroid or something else it would stop, change direction, accelerate, or decelerate, but in the absence of those forces it would just keep moving forever. On Earth we don't see this because the force of gravity and the friction of the air quickly prevents the softball from going too far before it hits the ground.

So, in summary, the first law explains that objects that are at rest remain at rest and objects in motion stay in their state of motion. This will be the case unless a force that is unbalanced acts on them to change their position or to accelerate them.

Here's one last example to think about. Suppose you have a heavy sofa, and you push toward the center and your friend is pushing on the other side at the same time. If you're both pushing with an equal amount of force, that sofa isn't going to budge. That's because there are two equal balanced forces pushing against each other. The sofa will only move if you are stronger than your friend and can push the sofa harder than he does.

Newton's second law of motion is about the relationship between force, mass and acceleration.

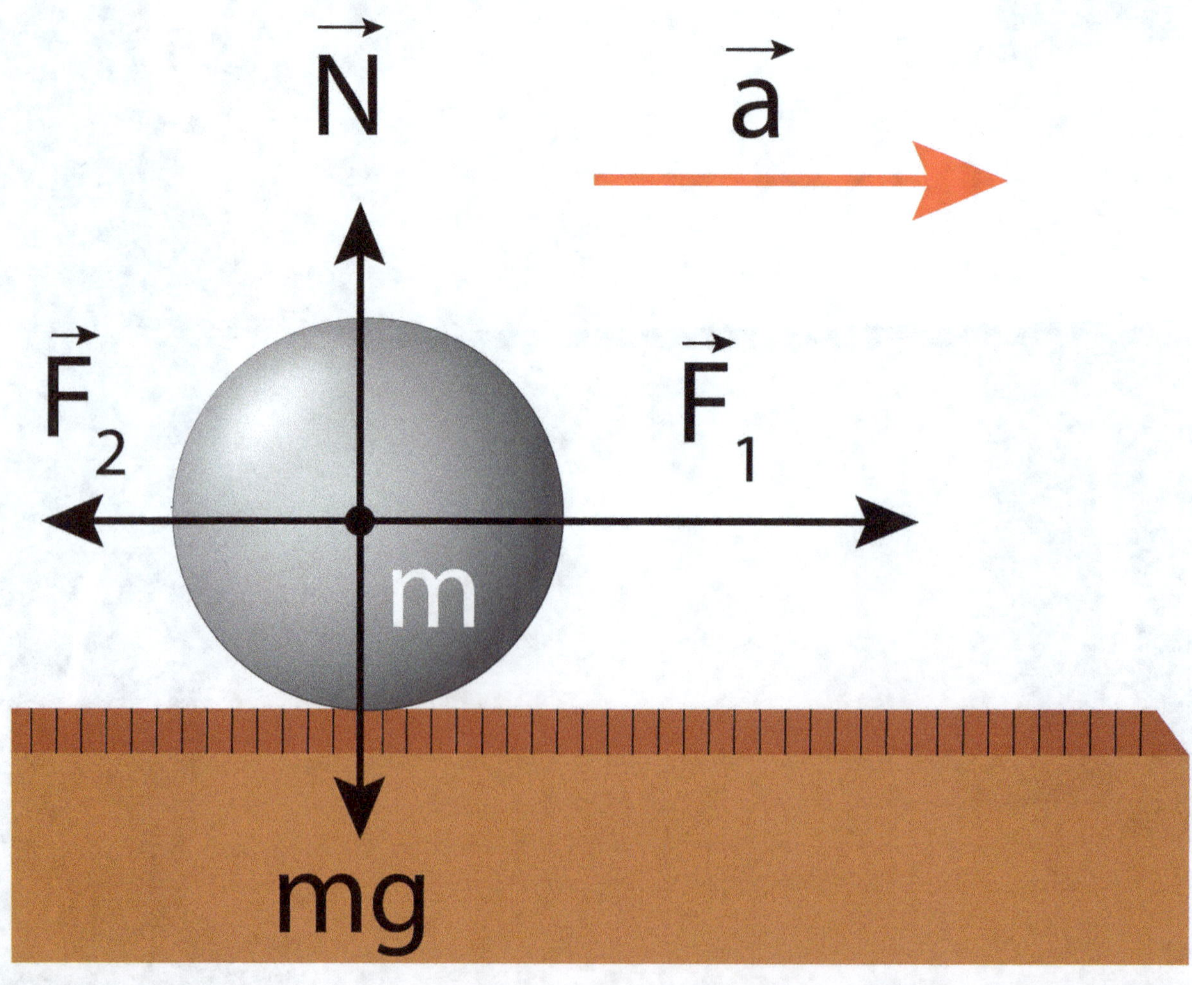

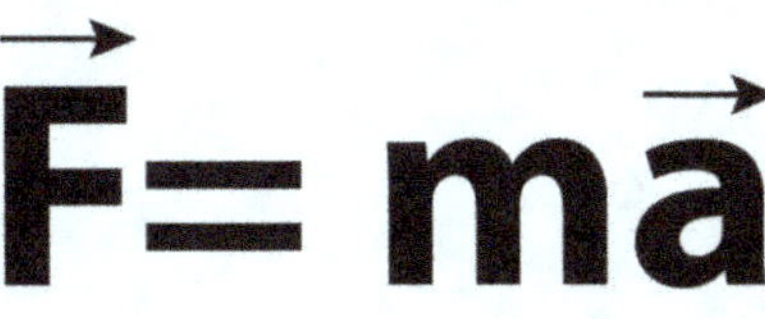

$\vec{F} = m\vec{a}$
$\vec{a}$
$\vec{F}$

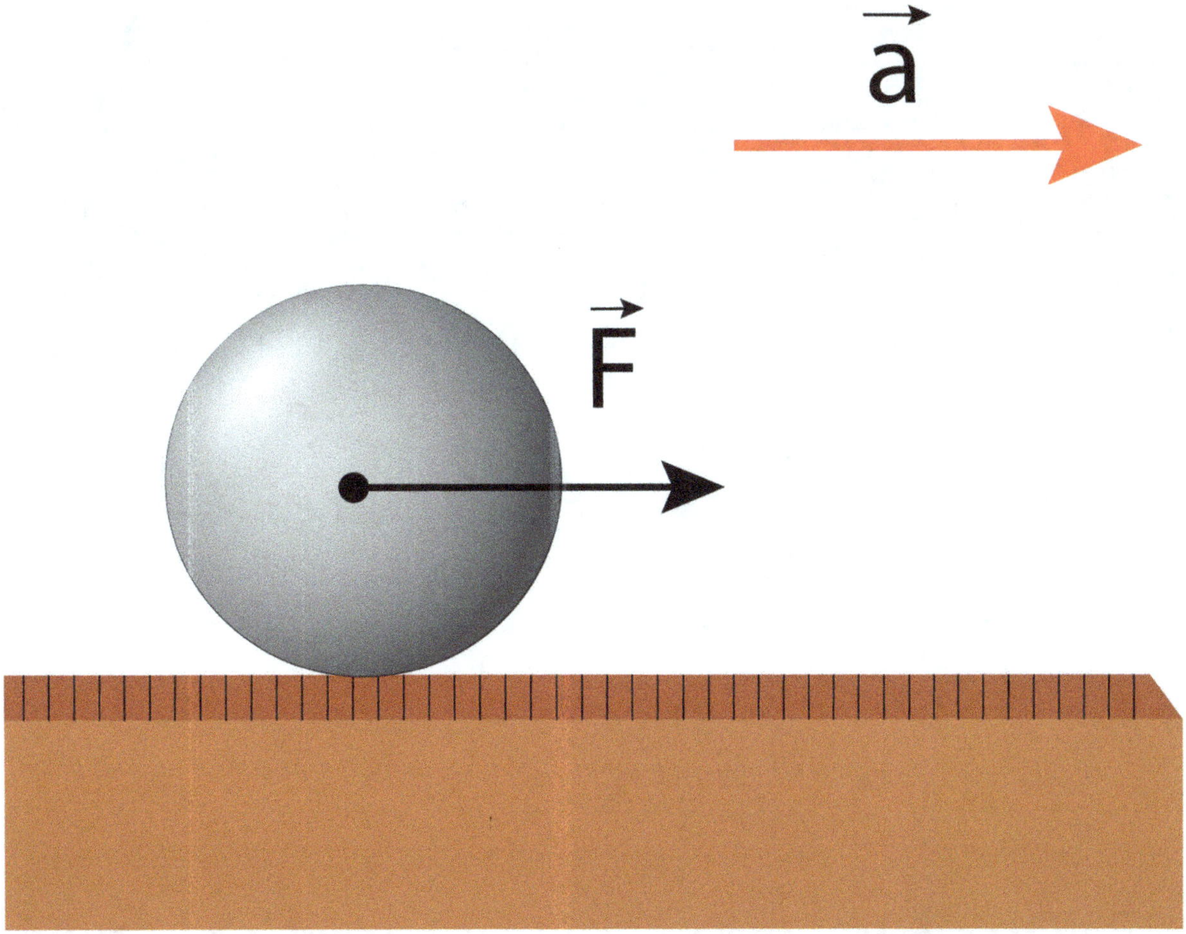

NEWTON'S SECOND LAW OF MOTION

Suppose you have a toy rocket and a real rocket. Which one is going to need more fuel to get it airborne and to have it accelerate or move faster once it gets a few feet above the surface?

This law seems clear. **The more mass an object has, the more force, it's going to take to get it to accelerate.** Newton expressed this with a very simple formula:

Force = mass x acceleration

$F = ma$, which is the same as $\dfrac{F}{m} = a$

In order to use this equation, mass is generally expressed in kilograms or kg, force is described in *Newtons*, abbreviated as **N**, and acceleration is expressed in meters per second squared or m/s^2.

PROBLEM: A box with a mass of 20 kilograms is resting on a very smooth tile floor. You kick the box across the floor with a force of 30 Newtons. What is the box's acceleration?

SOLUTION:

$$\frac{30 \text{ N}}{20 \text{ kg}} = 1.5 \text{ m/s}^2$$

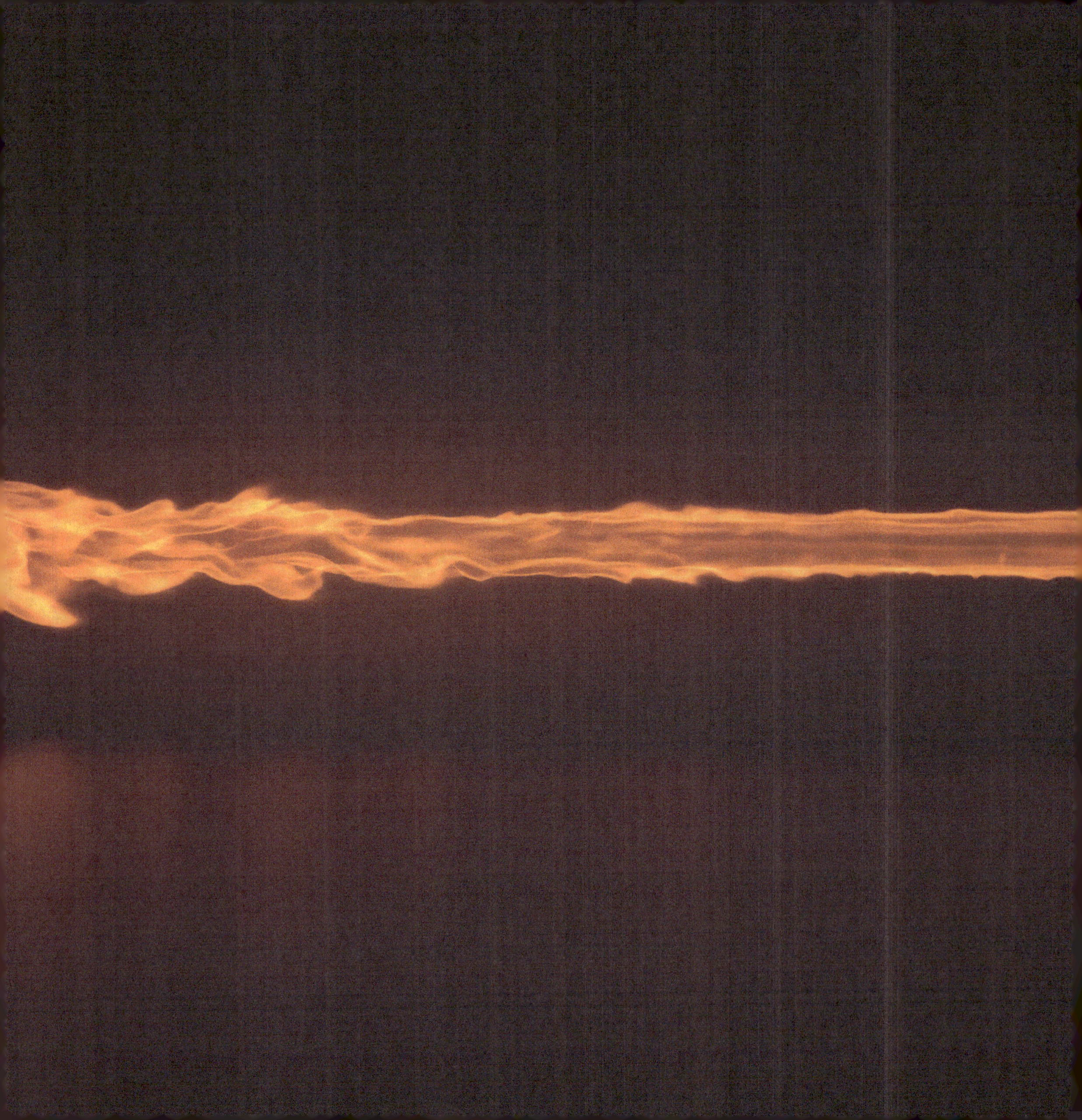

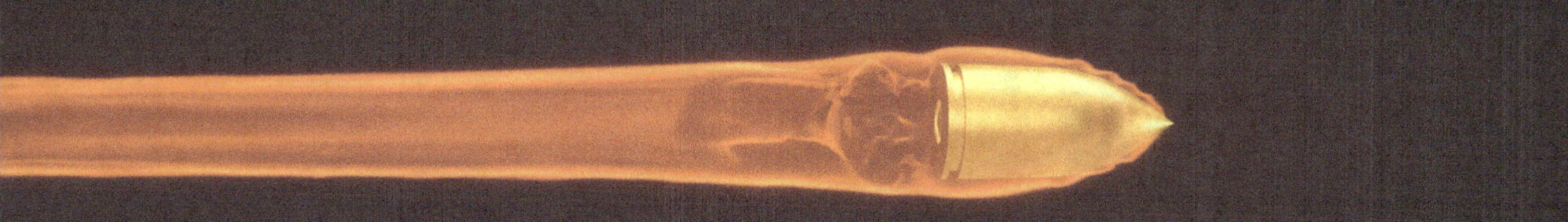

NEWTON'S THIRD LAW OF MOTION

Newton's third law tells us that forces come in pairs. For every action that takes place, there's an equal reaction that's its exact opposite. For example, if you fire a gun, the force and velocity of the bullet going out from the front of the gun, makes the gun recoil backwards. Another example is when a fish swims. A fish pushes the water backwards with its fins. The water pushes the fish forward with the same amount of force that the fish exerted in the other direction.

When a car is started and it begins to move, its wheels spin and gain traction on the road. This force, from the movement of the car, pushes on the road backwards. The force in the road exerts an equivalent force propelling the car forward. The result is that the car moves ahead on the road. This is why on roads with ice, cars skid and can't move forward because they have no traction.

Newton's 3rd Law.

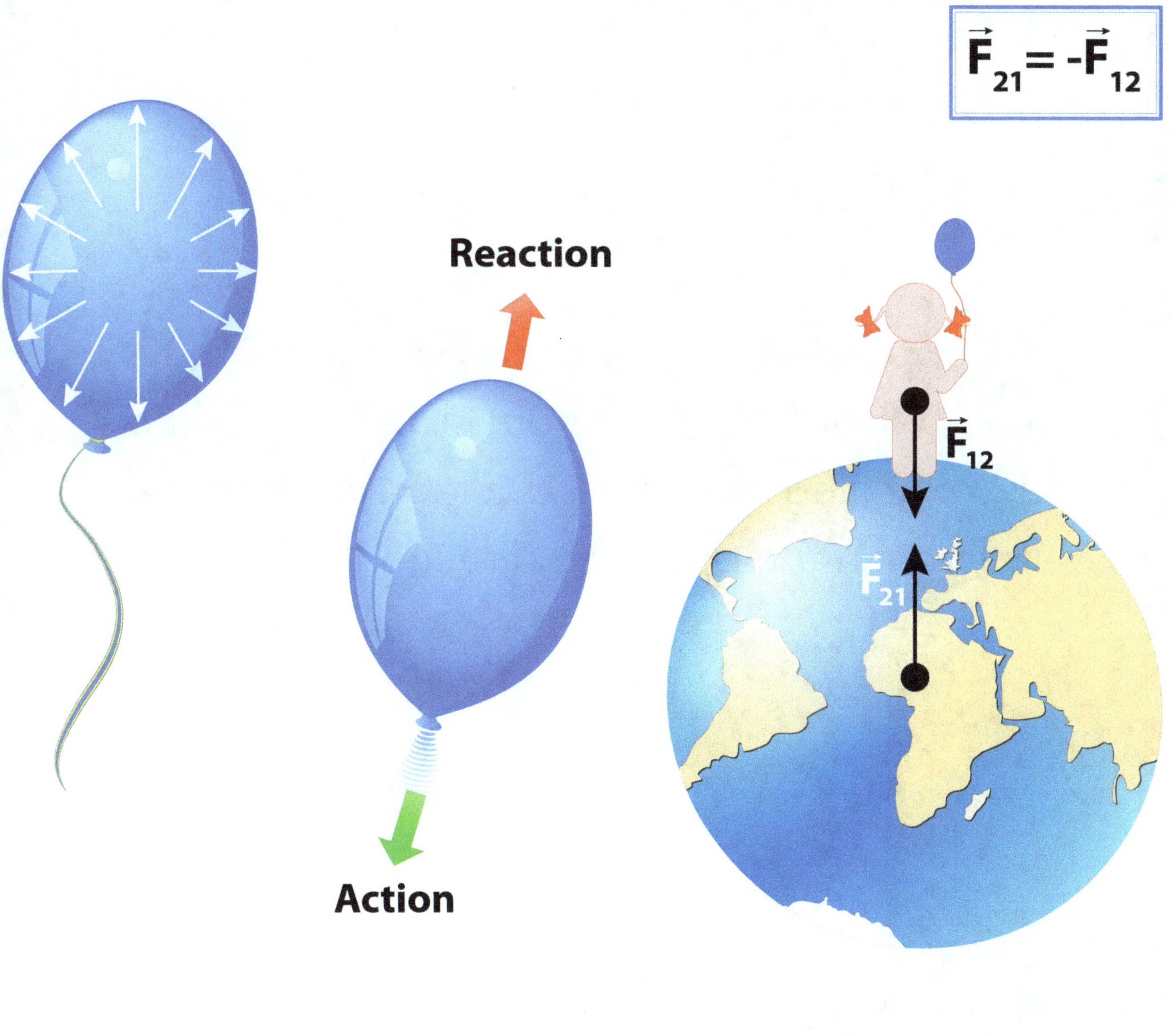

$$\vec{F}_{21} = -\vec{F}_{12}$$
Reaction
Action
$\vec{F}_{12}$
$\vec{F}_{21}$

Suppose you blow up a balloon with air. Then you let the air out. The force of the air expelling out of the balloon pushes the balloon in the opposite direction.

Awesome! Now you know more about Newton's Three Laws of Motion. You can find more Physics books from Baby Professor by searching the website of your favorite book retailer.

Visit
BABY PROFESSOR
EDUCATION KIDS
www.BabyProfessorBooks.com
to download Free Baby Professor eBooks
and view our catalog of new and exciting
Children's Books